Discovering
CHRISTMAS
CUSTOMS
AND
FOLKLORE

*A guide to
seasonal rites*

Margaret Baker

Shire Publications Ltd

CONTENTS

Copyright © 1968 and 1972 by Margaret Baker. First published 1968; reprinted 1970. Second edition 1972; reprinted 1976, 1979, 1982, 1984, 1986, 1989. Number 32 in the Discovering series. ISBN 0 85263 173 1.

Printed in Great Britain by C. I. Thomas & Sons (Haverfordwest) Ltd, Press Buildings, Merlins Bridge, Haverfordwest, Dyfed.

THE ORIGINS

Was 25th December really the birthday of Christ? No one knows. The early Christians celebrated Christmas (the Mass of Christ) on dates as widely apart as 1st and 6th of January, 29th March and 29th September. The firm choice of 25th December seems only to have been made by Pope Julius I (A.D. 337–52) and since the end of the fourth century this has been the date for the celebration of Christmas throughout Christendom.

But the choice of dates was not as arbitrary as it seems at first glance. It was a shrewd and practical decision on the part of the early church fathers, for mid-winter had always been a season of merry-making for many pagan peoples from whom the young Church intended to draw its converts. In Rome the 25th was observed as the *Dies Natalis Invicti Solis* (Birthday of the Unconquered Sun), sacred to Mithras, God of Light, and the Phrygian sun-god, Attis. The great Roman *Saturnalia,* a festival of fire and light, notorious for its wild celebrations, began on 17th December and lasted for seven days and this was quickly followed by the New Year celebrations of *Kalends*. As the Roman empire prospered and spread, these feasts had been carried to its remotest corners and the festivals were celebrated with as much enthusiasm on Hadrian's Wall as in the deserts of North Africa by the exiled Romans and their conquered peoples.

In the *Saturnalia* particularly all forms of anarchy, merriment and grotesque conduct were positively encouraged. Master and servant changed places or shared the same table, slaves wore their masters' clothes, lamps burned everywhere and greenery decorated the houses. At *Kalends* (which lasted for three days) gifts (called *strenae* since the goddess Strenia presided over the festival and greenery was brought from her groves for presents and decoration) were exchanged and divination told what the new year held in store. Wreaths and branches hung in the houses and the many rites included frolics through the streets by men with blackened faces who ran about dressed in animal skins, rites clearly perpetuated in the mumming plays.

In northern Europe, too, hard in the grip of icy winter, the solstice was celebrated by the festival of *Yule* with lights, evergreens in the houses, the making of gifts and, while fires blazed in the frosty air to the dark gods, Odin and Thor, the Wild Hunt (*Asgardereid*) could be heard in the winter storms

and the goddess Frey was worshipped. Mistletoe was ceremonially cut and sacrifices made, all in celebration of the turn
of the year when the sun, with its promise of light, heat,
spring, summer, crops, fertility and life, once again began to
climb the sky on 21st December.

Thus this was a season of established festival by the pagan
peoples of both north and south, whether Roman, Norsemen,
Celts or Teutons, and the Church prudently decided that
rather than attempt the impossible and suppress immemorial
custom amongst its growing flock it should weld Christmas to
Yule, Saturnalia and *Kalends* and make a new Christian
festival hallowed by special services and ritual.

Today this astonishing creation can still be seen in the
modern Christmas with its curious blend of Christian and
blatant pagan symbolism, with, in the twentieth century at
least, an ascendancy of the pagan and a frank and cheerful
acceptance of the true origins of the festival as a mid-winter
romp overlaid by a thin veneer of late-arriving Christian
ritual.

CHRISTMAS CUSTOMS AND CEREMONIES

The Christmas season has a rich variety of amusing
customs, many of which, if only in a revived or altered form,
can still be enjoyed by the spectator.

Every year, a few days before Christmas, it is the custom
of the Mayor of Glastonbury, Somerset, and the vicar of the
church of St. John the Baptist, to cut sprays from the world-
famous Glastonbury Thorn to be sent to the Queen for the
royal table on Christmas Day (plate 1). The story of the
custom is told and the letter which goes with the flowers is
read aloud to the crowd. A collect said to be associated with
St. Joseph of Arimathaea and other prayers are read.

The Glastonbury Thorn is perhaps the most famous tree in
Christendom. St. Joseph of Arimathaea is said to have visited
Glastonbury soon after the crucifixion to bring Christianity to
its people and to found the abbey. He planted his thorn staff
on the aptly named Weary-all Hill. It immediately rooted and
flowered and since then the tree (or rather its lineal descendant, for the original tree was destroyed by the Puritans as
idolatrous) flowers twice a year in the abbey grounds, including
Old Christmas Day, 6th January. The Puritan who actually
chopped down the older tree is said to have been blinded by
a flying chip. Slips of the tree were carried all over the world
by Bristol merchants and one enterprising Glastonbury man

raised a nursery of cuttings from the first tree which he sold for the high price of a crown each. In 1753 alterations in the calendar caused some difficulty and the *Gentleman's Magazine* wrote:

> Glastonbury—a vast concourse of people attended the noted thorns on Christmas-Day New-Stile, but to their great disappointment there was no appearance of its blowing, which made them watch it narrowly on the 6th January, the Christmas-Day, Old-Stile, when it blowed as usual.'

One of the earliest accounts of the tree was given in Hearne's *History and Antiquities of Glastonbury,* 1722, 'with an account of the Miraculous Thorn that blows still on Christmas Day' but there is apparently little documentary evidence before this date. Botanically the tree is *Crataegus monogyna praecox,* a type of hawthorn which flowers twice in the year and often once about Christmas time if the season is mild.

Another Holy Thorn, at Orcop, Herefordshire (perhaps a descendant of the Glastonbury Thorn) still receives many visitors who hope to see it bloom on 5th January. A Herefordshire correspondent wrote to *The Times* on 14th January

Bringing in the Yule log at Christmas Eve was an elaborate ceremony.

5

1949, saying that he had seen some of the buds open to full bloom within minutes of midnight on Old Christmas Eve.

The Yule log, with its suggestion of sparkling northern Christmases of the kind so seldom seen in England, is a delightful survival (though nowadays often only in the form of cakes or their decorations). This custom must have come over the North Sea with the Scandinavian invaders who kindled enormous bonfires at the winter solstice in honour of their gods. In the feudal period with its huge and hungry open fireplaces this became the most important Christmas custom and a carefully selected Yule log decorated with ribbons was dragged home from the woods in triumph. Anyone who met the procession raised his hat in salute for it was a sight full of good omens, not only a luck-bringer but a burner of old feuds and disputes and over it the wassail-bowl, drunk to the destruction of quarrels, bubbled merrily.

Ritually, on Christmas Eve, the log was lighted, but only by those with carefully washed hands for,

> Unwash't hands, ye maidens know,
> Dead the fire, though ye blow!

and after it had burned through the Twelve Days of Christmas the charred remains were carefully put away to kindle the log on the following year and in the meantime act as a charm to protect the house from fire and lightning. Herrick, with his intimate knowledge of the customs of Dean Prior, the Devon parish where he was a reluctant, if observant vicar, wrote:

> Come bring with noise,
> My merry, merry boys
> The Christmas log to the firing,
> While my good dame she,
> Bids ye all go free,
> And drink to your heart's desiring.
> With the last yeere's brand,
> Light the new block, and
> For your good successe in his spending,
> On your Psalteries play,
> That sweet luck may
> Come while the log is a-teending.
> Drink now the strong Beere,
> Cut the white loafe here,
> The while the meat is a-shredding:
> For the rare Mince-Pie
> And the Plums stand by
> To fill the paste that's a-kneading.

Dragging home the Yule log.

To fully conserve the luck certain requirements, rather like those of a first-footer, had to be met. No squinting person might enter the hall while the log was burning (which virtually condemned him to a solitary Christmas), no barefooted or, worst of all, flatfooted woman. Sometimes ash from the log was put aside to be mixed as a charm with the corn to be sown in the spring.

In Cornwall the Yule log was called the Mock and great festivities in true Celtic style accompanied the burning. Children were allowed to sit up till midnight on Christmas Eve to 'drink to the Mock'. In Devon the custom of the Ashen Faggot, very similar to the burning of the Yule log, continues. The ash tree has always been associated with witchcraft and divination was practised while it burned. The faggot was cut and bound with nine bands of green ash, from the same tree for preference: it was burned on the open fire and lighted with a fragment of last year's faggot. The unmarried girls

7

of the household would each choose a band and wait for it to burst in the heat: the person whose band burst first would be first to marry. While the faggot blazed rank was forgotten on many Devon farms, while master and servant enjoyed the warmth together and the cider flowed freely. This custom is still carried on at the Luttrell Arms Hotel, Dunster, Somerset, where the faggot is lighted at 7 p.m. on Christmas Eve and, as was the custom in inns, a fresh round of cider is drunk each time a band breaks.

Wassailing the apple tree is another West Country custom which was also observed in other fruit-growing areas such as Herefordshire and indeed is still practised. It usually takes place on Twelfth Night, or sometimes on Old Twelfth Night (17th January). In Devon the farmer and his family ate hot cakes and cider, then adjourned to the orchard after dark carrying further supplies. A cake soaked in cider was laid on the fork of the tree and cider thrown over as a libation. The men then fired guns into the tree and banged on pots, pans or kettles, while the company solemnly bowed and sang the *Wassail Song* with the words:

> Bear blue, apples and pear enow,
> Barn fulls, bag fulls, sack fulls,
> Hurrah! Hurrah! Hurrah!

In Norfolk, Wiltshire and the New Forest similar ceremonies took place and here they sang:

> Apples and pears with right good corn,
> Come in plenty to every one,
> Eat and drink good cake and hot ale,
> Give Earth to drink and she'll not fail.

while spiced ale was generously sprinkled over the orchard and surrounding meadows. These customs (sometimes known as apple-howling, as well as wassailing) seem plainly intended to drive the bad spirits from the orchard and to encourage the kindly vegetation spirits to provide a plentiful harvest in the following year. The custom still continues at Carhampton, near Minehead, Somerset, on Old Twelfth Night, where the song:

> Old apple tree, old apple tree
> We've come to wassail thee.

is sung (plate 6).

In Yorkshire 'gooding' (sometimes called 'doleing' or 'mumping') was an accepted custom. Children went round the villages on begging expeditions singing the following song and carrying a Christmas tree as a badge:

8

The Lord of Misrule and his page acted as masters of ceremonies for the twelve days of Christmas.

Well-a-day! Well-a-day!
Christmas too soon goes away,
Then your gooding we do pray,
For the goodtime will not stay,
We are not beggars from door to door,
But neighbours' children known before
So gooding, pray,
We cannot stay,
But must away,
For the Christmas will not stay,
Well-a-day! Well-a-day!

The considerable psychological cunning of these words no doubt brought worth-while results. An even plainer song was sung at Harrington, Worcestershire:

Wassail, wassail, through the town,
If you've got any apples throw them down,
Up with the stocking and down with the shoe,
If you've got no apples, money will do.

At Kingscote, Gloucestershire, the wassailers were accompanied by a man with his head thrust into a bull's mask and the Christmas Bull, with his keeper, was allowed into every house. The Hodening Horse went round villages with an attendant band of boys, prancing and dancing at every door. His body was covered with a white sheet and his jaws could open and shut realistically. In some districts Hodening was a Christmas custom while in others it took place on All Souls' Day. In Wales the custom of Mari Lwyd (Grey Mare or Grey Mary and perhaps a survival of a medieval religious drama) still continues at Pencoed, near Maesteg, Glamorgan, in which a horse's skull decorated with ribbons and with bottle-glass eyes, is carried round on a long pole by a man hidden under a white cloth, accompanied by a party including the stock characters, Leader, Merryman, Punch and Judy and Sergeant. Again the jaws can open and shut and the figure chases and bites everyone it can catch, releasing its victim only on payment of a forfeit.

On 21st December, St. Thomas's Day, the winter solstice ('St. Thomas Gray, St. Thomas Gray, Longest night and shortest day') is a favourite day for the payment of charities. In Warwickshire the poor of the villages visited the farmers 'a-corning' (also called 'Thomassing'), collecting flour with which to bake a special batch of Christmas bread. In return householders received a sprig of holly. A candle auction conducted by the vicar takes place at Bolingbroke, Lincolnshire, on St. Thomas's Day. He sticks a pin into a lighted candle and accepts bids for the grazing rights on a piece of land let for charity. The last bid received before the pin falls decides the tenant of the land for the following year. Another candle auction is held every three years in the village hall at Aldermaston in Berkshire, at 8 p.m., about 13th December and they were once common in a number of other villages. Another St. Thomas's Day custom was for schoolchildren to bar the schoolmaster from the school if they could reach it first in the morning.

The now defunct custom of electing a Boy Bishop seems to have been an interesting link with the anarchical atmosphere of the *Saturnalia*. This ceremony, which now only survives in a revived and expurgated form, was one of the oldest rituals of the medieval church, an extraordinary mixture of the sacred and burlesque. A boy chosen from the choir attached to the church was ordained 'Bishop' and wore the full vestments of a real bishop. The election took place on St. Nicholas's Day (6th December) and his tenure of office extended until Holy Innocents' Day (28th December), and during this period the boy preached and was allowed to perform all the offices of bishop with the exception of mass. If the boy died during the period he was buried with full honours as though he had been a real bishop and Salisbury Cathedral has an effigy of a boy bishop in full vestments, who died under these circumstances.

The office was abolished during the reign of Henry VIII, revived and again abolished in the Elizabethan period. Various revivals have taken place since. In 1965 at Clutton, Bristol, this took place and the 'Bishop' takes a part in the services and preaches a sermon during his term of office.

Tolling the Devil's Knell takes place at Dewsbury, Yorkshire, on Christmas Eve; it has been rung regularly for over seven hundred years. The knell, which is pulled for the same number of years as have elapsed since the birth of Christ, is supposed to celebrate the Devil's departure from the earth (and more specifically, from Dewsbury). In 1975 the bell was tolled 1,975 times, beginning at 11 p.m. The bell used is called Black Tom of Soothill and is named after Thomas de Soothill who is said to have presented a bell to the church as a penance for having killed one of his servants in the thirteenth century (plate 14).

In Cheshire farmers once had an uncomfortable and busy Christmas, for farm servants in the county would only bind themselves from New Year's Day to Christmas Day, thus ensuring several days' holiday at the end of their service. The streets of Chester were thronged with farm workers (to the delight of the shopkeepers) dressed in their best, with their pockets full of a year's wages, while the farmers had to work doubly hard to cover their absence.

The Haxey Hood Game, played at Haxey, Humberside, on 6th January, may be far older than it seems and is one of the most interesting Christmas survivals. The story told, which seems to have been added to rationalise an older tradition, is that Lady Mowbray was riding from Haxey church one day in the thirteenth century when her hood blew away in the wind and was gallantly retrieved by twelve labourers. She was grateful and as a reward arranged to give a piece of land called Hoodlands, the rent from which was to provide a hood to be competed for each Old Christmas Day by twelve men in red jerkins. Even today the players wear something red on their clothing. The players are known as Boggans (plate 7) and are led by the King Boggan and accompanied by the Fool with blackened face, who stands on a stone to announce the rules of the game. While he is doing this the paper strips hanging from his hat are set on fire and this is known as Smoking the Fool. The game begins and the hood, now a rolled-up piece of leather, is put into play. Nowadays the players come from three local pubs and the hood is kept in the victors' bar until the following year. The whole ritual seems to be far older than Lady Mowbray and may be a pagan spring rite with the hood representing part of a sacrificed animal (Old Danish for head is *huid,* from which the word hood may be derived). The smoking perhaps recalls a human sacrifice.

CHRISTMAS FOLKLORE AND SUPERSTITION

The folklore and superstition of Christmas forms one of the richest fields a storiologist could wish to plough, for the antiquity of many of its beliefs, which must have been preserved perhaps only in half-comprehension for thousands of years, is perfectly plain.

Many are associated with fertility and good fortune. In Derbyshire and Devonshire they say that if the sun shines through the apple trees on Christmas Day there will be an abundant crop next autumn. The preservation of a small piece of charred Yule log at the end of the Christmas season would protect the house from fire and lightning and a Yule candle left burning through Christmas Eve will bring good luck in the coming year. At St. John's College, Oxford, a huge candle burned on the high table at supper for all the twelve days of Christmas. At one time specially large candles were made for this season (and were sometimes sent by grocers to their customers as seasonal gifts) to be lighted by the head of the household and ritually extinguished later. If the candle went out by accident bad luck would surely follow.

Some beliefs were associated with animals, crops and natural occurrences. Bees are said to hum the Hundredth Psalm in their hives at midnight on Christmas Eve and farm animals speak amongst themselves, but any attempt to overhear what they say is highly dangerous. A very common belief is that cattle turn to the east at midnight on Christmas Eve and bow (in Herefordshire only seven-year-old cattle do this since this was the age of the cattle at Bethlehem) and in some districts conservative cattle bowed on Old Christmas Eve (5th January) and ignored the calendar alterations of 1752. This was taken, with the blooming of the Holy Thorn at Glastonbury and elsewhere, to show that 6th January was indeed the true date for Christmas, whatever the reformers might ordain. Since a cock was said to have been the first to proclaim Christ's birth by crying *Christus Natus Est,* cocks now crow through Christmas Eve and even weathercocks may join in. Any dog which howled then was shot at once, for it was said that the animal would certainly go mad before the new year was out.

More domestically, bread baked on Christmas Eve or Day was a good remedy for diarrhoea and dysentery and generally magical and healing (hardly surprising after the gargantuan meals which lay ahead). Sometimes it was dried and powdered and put away for future use. In Oxfordshire a single girl would bake a *Dumb Cake* while fasting on Christmas Eve, prick it with her initials and leave it on the hearthstone. At midnight her future husband's double would enter the room, add his initials and leave. The door must be left open for him and if, by accident, it was closed, the results would be dire. Sit under a pine tree on Christmas Eve to hear the angels sing but remember that the benefit must be balanced against the inevitable early death of the hearer. Never make a besom broom during the Twelve Days.

Returning spirits favoured the Christmas season. The house must be left clean for them and everything prepared for Christmas before the family left for church. While the house was empty the spirits would come and inspect the house and perhaps take a meal. To please them meant a successful year.

In Lincolnshire a child born on Christmas Day was especially favoured and gifted (Sir Isaac Newton born at Woolsthorpe, Lincolnshire, on Christmas Day 1642, bore this out) and would have psychic powers. In Berkshire, according to a correspondent to *Notes and Queries*, 1859, a watcher on Christmas Eve would hear subterranean bells and in mining areas the workmen declared that high mass was performed during this night by unseen choristers in the mine with the richest lode of ore, which was lighted supernaturally during the service.

The weather, too, was carefully watched for portents and gave rise to many sayings. Thomas Passenger, who lived at the Three Bibles and Star on Old London Bridge, had a great reputation for his popular histories and chapbooks at the end of the seventeenth century and brought out the *Shepherd's Kalendar*, full of weather lore. 'If New Year's Day, in the morning, open with dusky red clouds, it denotes strifes and debates amongst great ones and many robberies to happen that year' (prognostications fairly certain to be fulfilled with or without the influence of the weather, one feels). 'If the sun shine clear and bright on Christmas Day, it promiseth a peacable year from clamours and strife, and foretells much plenty to ensue: but if the wind blow stormy toward sunset, it betokeneth sickness in the spring and autumn quarters'. A manuscript of 1699 added that '31st December, of which day Judas was born, who betrayed Christ, is a dangerous day to begin any business, fall sick, or undertake any journey'. And R. Inwards in *Weather Lore*, 1869, added 'if the ice will bear a man before Christmas it will not bear a goose after'.

CHRISTMAS FOOD AND DRINK

The boar's head was always a favourite dish in England and was especially associated with Christmas. At the Scandinavian festival of *Yule* it was eaten in honour of the Sun-Boar and was a dish sacred to the heroes of Valhalla. Sometimes vows were taken over the dish during the meal. In medieval England it was carried into the great hall on a silver or gold dish to the sound of trumpets at the head of a procession of lords, knights and ladies who sang:

Caput apri defero,
Reddens laudes Domino,
The boar's head in hand bring I
With garland gay and rosemary,
I pray you all sing merrily,
Qui estis in convivio.

Be glad both more or less,
For thus hath ordained our steward,
To cheer you all this Christmas—
The boar's head and mustard.

The decorated boar's head, with an apple, orange or lemon in its teeth, was related to the pig sacrificed to the goddess of fertility, Frey, and the mustard was so essential a condiment that in the time of the Commonwealth, when Christmas was threatened with extinction, the mustard-makers complained bitterly that they could find no sale for their wares. After the Restoration the boar's head revived in popularity once again but never quite regained its place of former glory on the Christmas menu.

At Queen's College, Oxford, the boar's head ceremony continues and the head is carried in on a silver meat dish presented to the college in 1668 by Sir Joseph Williamson, gaily decorated with holly, bay, mistletoe and rosemary and with an orange between its teeth (plate 8). Ahead walk

Bringing in the boar's head. An illustration by Ralph Caldecott from 'Old Christmas, from the Sketch Book of Washington Irving', 1882.

trumpeters and the choir who sing the Boar's Head Carol in which the company joins:

> The Boar's Head in hand bear I,
> Bedeck'd with bays and rosemary,
> And I pray you my masters be merry,
> Quot estis in convivio.
> Caput apri defero,
> Reddens laudes Domino.

(a slight variant of the version given above). The chief singer receives the orange from the Provost while the sprigs of rosemary are presented to the fellows and guests. During the Second World War tradition continued—but with a boar's head made of papier mâché! At Hurstpierpoint College, Sussex, the choir led by a boy carrying a mustard pot precedes the Cantor and the head is carried on a large dish by four boys. At the end of the procession comes the cook ready with carving knife and steel. The Cutlers Company of London hold a similar ceremony on 16th December with the Boar's Head Carol sung by the choirboys of St. Paul's Cathedral.

Geese, capons, pheasant, bustards, swans, pickled oysters and, above all, peacocks, were almost equally important. The peacock would be carefully skinned and the plumage set aside intact. The bird was roasted, the feathers replaced, the beak gilded and the bird went to table. The serving fell to the most distinguished ladies present, either by birth or beauty.

The now-supreme turkey was a later arrival. As the old rhyme says:

> Turkey, Carpes, Picarel and Beer,
> Came into England all in one year.

which was about 1518 and by 1542 the turkey appeared regularly on the English Christmas table. Great flocks were kept in Norfolk and Suffolk, then as now, and driven to London slowly as the Christmas season approached, stopping to graze and rest by the roadside verges during their long journey.

A traditional custom is for two people to hold each end of the merry-thought or wishbone from the carcase of game or poultry, to wish and to pull. As the bone breaks the person with the longer piece (in some districts the shorter) will gain his wish, but only if he does not reveal his thoughts or laugh and talk during the proceedings.

Mince-pies or Christmas pies (sometimes called mutton pies or shred pies) from which the modern mince-pie is derived, were often made with an oval pastry crust said to

Norman Heal

1. Cutting the Glastonbury thorn is an annual ceremony. The sprays are sent to the Queen for the royal table on Christmas Day (see page 4).

2. Christmas masque at the court of Charles II. This Victorian engraving shows Father Christmas and mummers carrying the wassail bowl.

3. Mummers performing a play in the village inn. H the various characters, including the traditional Harley Street doctor, parad around the room (see pa 46).

4. 'Bringing home the Christmas tree', by Alfred Hunt, from 'Illustrated London News', 1882 (see page 41).

R. D. Barrett-Lennard

5. *The traditional ceremony of blessing the plough on Plough Sunday in January, at Chichester cathedral (see page 55).*

6. *Wassailers at Carhampton, Somerset, fire their guns into the apple trees on Twelfth Night (see page 8).*

Brian Shuel

Doncaster Evening Post

7. Participants in the Haxey Hood Game are known as Boggans
(see page 12).

8. *The decorated and beflagged boar's head from the ceremony at Queen's College, Oxford (see page 15).*

9. *Each year the people of Oslo in Norway present a Christmas tree to London. It stands, illuminated, in Trafalgar Square (see page 42).*

10. 'Burning the Christmas greens', from 'Harper's Weekly', 1876
(see page 29).

THE WASSAIL BOWL.

" DROP PARTY SPIRIT QUITE,
  'TIS HEAVY, HEADY, STUFF,
ALL MEN *PUNCH* DOTH INVITE
  TO TIPPLE *QUANTUM SUFF*:
    OF HIS WASSAIL !"

" GOOD LUCK BETIDE YOU ALL !
  ONE BUMPER MORE WE'LL FILL ;
PUNCH HOPES, AND EVER SHALL,
  FOR PEACE AND FOR GOOD-WILL,
    THAT'S HIS WASSAIL !"

11. 'The Wassail Bowl', from 'Punch', 29th December 1888 (see page 27).

represent the manger in which Christ was laid. Hone's *Table Book* quotes a pie made for Sir Henry Grey with two bushels of flour and twenty pounds of butter for the pastry and four geese, two turkeys, four ducks, as well as rabbits, curlews, blackbirds, pigeons, partridges, snipe, woodcock and tongues, forming the mixture inside. It was this form of Christmas pie into which Little Jack Horner (plate 13) put his thumb. Various explanations have been made of this rhyme. One story told is that Jack Horner was steward to Abbot Whiting, last abbot of Glastonbury who, anxious for his prospects at the time of the Dissolution of the Monasteries, sent Henry VIII a handsome Christmas present of a large pie, dispatched to London in Horner's keeping. On the way, Jack, either from hunger or curiosity, investigated the pie and found it contained the deeds of twelve Somersetshire manors, including the Manor of Mells, as a softening-up present. It is said that Horner helped himself to the deeds of Mells and it is true that the manor shortly afterwards passed into the hands of the Horner family who still own it. Leland's *Itinerary,* supported by the family, maintain that it was legally purchased but perhaps there is some justification for the story since a Thomas Horner was on the jury which condemned Abbot Whiting when he was finally brought to trial. The Horners were King's Men and perhaps the opening of the pie and the acquiring of the deeds was a euphemism for getting them by trickery. As early as 1690 a Somerset rhyme ran:

> Hopton, Horner, Smyth and Thynne,
> When the Abbots went out, they came in.

which adds weight to the tradition of the strangest of Christmas presents.

In some places it was regarded as unlucky to refuse an offered mince-pie, however many had been eaten already, for it was a token rejection of good fortune and plenty. But to eat a mince-pie on each of the Twelve Days of Christmas would ensure twelve happy months ahead. As each pie was eaten the toast 'Happy Month' was said. Sometimes the charm would work if twelve pies were eaten over the Christmas season and not necessarily day-by-day. The Puritans particularly disliked them and eventually the idea developed that it was disgraceful for a clergyman even to be seen eating them. Gradually the mixture used for the pies was changed from savoury to sweet and now consists of raisins, sugar, peel, almonds, suet, apples and very occasionally a little chopped meat, now the only link with the earlier Christmas pie.

Cakes, sweetmeats, nuts, gingerbread and march pane (the name comes from the French *marce pain,* although it is more usually known by its German form of marzipan) were other items in the Christmas feast. As early as 1615 Markham's *English Housewife* was saying, 'To make the best Marchpane, take the best Jordan Almonds'. Plum-porridge or plum-pottage was another favourite which finally fell out of fashion early in the nineteenth century. This was usually served with the first course of the Christmas dinner and was made by boiling beef and mutton with broth thickened with breadcrumbs, raisins, currants, and prunes and seasoned with wine, spices, cloves and ginger and sent to the table in a semi-liquid state to be eaten with a spoon with the meat course. From this grew the stiffer, modern Christmas pudding, popular from about 1670. The Sunday nearest to St. Andrew's Day is called Stir-Up Sunday (supposedly from the collect for the day 'Stir up, we beseech Thee, O Lord, the wills of thy faithful people') and this was the traditional day for Christmas pudding making and stirring. Schoolboys went round the houses singing:

Stir up, we beseech thee,
The pudding in the pot,
And when we get home,
We'll eat the lot.

Frumenty, in some places a ritual food eaten first on Christmas morning and last at night, was made in the following way: 'Take clean wheat and bray it in a mortar, that the hulls be all gone off, and seethe it till it burst, and take it up and let it cool, and take clean fresh broth, and sweet milk of almonds, or sweet milk of kine and temper it all, and take the yolks of eggs. Boil it a little, and set it down and mess it forth with venison or fresh mutton'. Venison was seldom served without this accompaniment and frumenty was often eaten too, on its own and sweetened with sugar.

Festive drinks were of the greatest importance. In Devon egg-hot (cider heated and mixed with spices and eggs) was drunk while the Yule log blazed. In some places ale posset (hot milk, ale, sugar and spices) was the final drink on Christmas Eve.

Lambswool was another standard Christmas drink and the custom of making it has been revived in some City of London taverns where the ceremony of Hoisting the Ale Garland takes place. The City Ale Conners attend this pleasant ceremony in their official robes and sample the brew. If the verdict is favourable the garland is hoisted and the company

*The wassail-bowl, drawn by Ralph Caldecott for 'Old
Christmas, from the Sketch Book of Washington Irving', 1882.*

enjoys the drink. Lambswool is a mixture of ale, roasted
apples, sugar, spices, eggs, thick cream and snippets of bread.
In Gloucestershire a wassail-bowl containing it was carried
round the town to the song:

> Wassail! Wassail! All over the town,
> Our toast is white, our ale is brown,
> Our bowl is made of the maplin tree,
> We be good fellows: I drink to thee!

and blessings were called on the master and mistress of the
household and their children. Jesus College, Oxford, has a
ten-gallon silver-gilt wassail-bowl for this drink and in the
Shetland Isles the traditional drink of egg-yolks beaten with
sugar and cream, with brandy added and called Whipcoll,
is similar.

A deliciously expansive recipe for making up the wassail-
bowl in the nineteenth century ran:

> 'Simmer a small quantity of the following spices in a tea-
> cupful of water, viz: Cardamums, cloves, nutmeg, mace,
> ginger, cinamon and coriander. When done, put the spice
> to two, four or six bottles of port, sherry, or madeira, with
> one pound and a half of fine loaf sugar (pounded) to
> four bottles, and set all on the fire in a clean bright
> saucepan: meanwhile, have yolks of 12 and the whites

of 6 eggs well whisked up in it. Then, when the spice
and sugared wine is a little warm, take out one teacupful
and so on for three or four cups: after which, when
boils, add the whole of the remainder, pouring it i
gradually, and stirring it briskly all the time, so as t
froth it. The moment a fine froth is obtained toss in 1
fine soft roasted apples, and send it up hot.'

Punch was another excuse for the wildest extravagance
The name was said by the Indian traveller Fryer in 1672 t
come from the Hindu for five—panch—a reference to i
five ingredients, but it seems to have been well known befor
this date. Sir Edward Kennel, the Commander-in-Chief o
the English Navy, made a huge punch for his ships' crews on
25th October 1599, in a vast marble bowl. He used 80 cask
of brandy, 9 casks of water, 25,000 limes, 80 pints of lemo
juice, 1300 pounds of sugar, 5 pounds of nutmeg and 30
biscuits together with a large cask of Malaga. This serve
6000 guests and was served by the ships' boys. The fume
were so powerful that the boys had to be replaced ever
fifteen minutes. Now punch is usually a mixture of wine o
spirits, sugar, lemon juice, cloves and spices and hot water.

An early Christmas card by W. M. Egley c. 1845.

CHRISTMAS GREENERY AND DECORATIONS

The Roman and Norse customs of decorating with ever-greens, life-symbols, fresh, green and magically fruiting in mid-winter, were joyfully embraced by the early Christians. Greenery brought into the house at the winter solstice seemed to be a charm to ensure the return of vegetation to the earth, and later John Stow in his *Survey of London,* 1598, wrote, 'Against the time of Christmas, every man's house, as also their parish churches, were decked with holme, ivie, bayes and whatsoever the season affordeth to be greene'. Street standards and conduits were decorated as well as houses and wreaths on doors are not as modern as they seem.

The use of evergreens was hemmed in with a great profusion of prohibitions. It was unlucky to bring them into the house before Christmas Eve or to take them down before Twelfth Night, which fecklessly threw away their intrinsic good fortune. Disposal was very difficult. In some districts they must be burned (plate 10), in others burning was unlucky—they must be left to wither and the burning of green holly (although its survival after twelve days in a warm house was improbable) was foolish to a degree. Sometimes a sprig was kept back to carry the luck forward over the coming year. Decorations might remain in churches until the end of the ecclesiastical Christmas season (Candlemas) but they too must go before the 2nd February and every leaf overlooked had its burden of ill-luck. Herrick wrote of his Devon village:

> Down with the rosemary and so,
> Down with the baies and mistletoe,
> Down with the holly, ivie, all,
> Wherewith ye drest the Christmas hall.
>
> That so the superstitious find
> Not one least branch there left behind,
> For look, how many leaves there be,
> Neglected there, maids trust to me
> So many goblins you shall see.

Mistletoe was one of the most magical plants known to men (especially if growing on the oak) and significantly banned from churches (although essential in the house) because of its pagan associations. Even now many observant vicars banish the smallest sprig. It was used in both the summer and winter solstice celebrations and protected houses from thunder, lightning, spells and evil of all kinds. In

Scandinavia, too, it was the plant of peace, which hung outside the house as an expression of hospitality and welcome within.

In Worcestershire, a good county for it, it is said to be unlucky to cut mistletoe at any time other than Christmas and until recently (perhaps still) a bunch was preserved through the year to carry on the good magic. In some country districts a sprig was fed to the first cow to calve after New Year's Day to bring good health to the herd in the year ahead. To cut down a mistletoe-bearing tree meant a particularly unpleasant end for the destroyer but mistletoe laid on a cradle protected the child within from the influence of fairies and from the risk of being a changeling. In Staffordshire they kept a bunch to burn under next year's Christmas pudding or hung a sprig round the neck to repel witches.

Mistletoe is a European hemiparasitic plant (*Viscum album*) common on the apple from the Baltic to the Mediterranean, found too, on poplars, hawthorns, limes and maples, rarely on oaks and even less commonly on pears, but with a high reputation as a medicinal plant. It was the Golden Bough of classical legend which Aeneas picked from the oak at the gate of the underworld and it was the slayer of Baldur the Sun-God. Medicinally it was the All-Heal, useful in epilepsy, St. Vitus' Dance, heart disease, unspecified nervous illnesses, sores, snakebite and toothache and had a useful psychological reputation as a composer of quarrels. Modern research has proved these ancient beliefs correct for the plant contains the drug guipsine, now known to be useful in the treatment of hypertension and nervous illnesses. It was once used, too, in the preparation of flypapers, because of its sticky quality.

The Druids cut it ceremonially with a golden sickle and the falling shrub must not touch the ground as it fell but had to be caught in their robes, while two white bulls were ceremonially sacrificed. Mistletoe was also a sexual symbol and the ritual plucking is said to symbolise the emasculation of the old king by his successor. Kissing under the mistletoe may be a shadowy recollection of its sexual significance. Despite our national reputation for coolness this seems to be an entirely English custom. Visiting foreigners have always been surprised (if not alarmed) by our freedom in kissing and even the placid Erasmus wrote, 'Wherever you go, everyone welcomes you with a kiss'. Chamber's *Book of Days*, 1864, commented, 'A branch of the mystic plant is suspended from the wall or ceiling and any one of the fair sex who, either from inadvertence, or as possibly may be insinuated, *on purpose*, passes beneath the sacred spray incurs the penalty of being

Phiz's sketch of Christmas Eve at Mr. Wardle's, from Dickens' 'Pickwick Papers'.

then and there kissed by any lord of creation who chooses to avail himself of the privilege'. In some places mistletoe is burned after Twelfth Night in case the boys and girls who kissed under it never marry.

A curious exception to its exclusion from churches was the custom of carrying a great branch of it in procession to the high altar of York Minster (perhaps a last link with the freedom of the Roman *Saturnalia* in a draughty outpost of Roman Empire) when a general pardon was proclaimed until its removal on Twelfth Night.

31

The holly (*Ilex aquifolium*) with its handsome shining leaves and scarlet berries was another symbol of eternal life, valued for its winter fruiting and useful for treating fevers, dropsy and rheumatism, gout and asthma. The North American Indians used holly tea in the treatment of measles. An unpleasant English recipe for the treatment of worms advised the patient to yawn over a dish of sage and holly leaves in water, whereupon the worms would drop out of his mouth.

Holly had many associations with good fortune. In Louisiana berries were kept for luck and animals are known to thrive if a piece of holly is hung in the cowshed on Christmas Eve. A piece kept back from church decorations was especially lucky. Unlike mistletoe, holly was perfectly acceptable in churches and a tree planted outside the house protected it from thunder, lightning, fire and the evil eye. Can this be the true reason for the proliferation of Holly Cottages across England?

The common holly had male associations because of its prickly leaves and was a symbol for men while the smooth, variegated type (she-holly) was a feminine symbol. To induce dreams of one's future mate, gather nine she-holly leaves in silence at midnight on a Friday and tie them with nine knots in a three-cornered handkerchief. Place this under your pillow and by preserving silence from the time of plucking till the following morning the desired person will appear in your dreams. A cruel Derbyshire remedy for chilblains was to thrash them with holly—'to let the chilled blood out'—which may have restored the circulation but was really a true survival of the magical ritual of flagellation. In Wales holly taken into the house before Christmas Eve can lead to family quarrels, and for medicinal purposes holly picked on Christmas Day was especially powerful. It was inviting disaster to burn green holly or to stamp on the berries or even to bring holly flowers into the house in summer.

Ivy was a kindly plant, a feminine life-symbol with its clinging habits, and used in conjunction with holly would bring fertility to the whole household. The early Christians frowned on the plant because of its Bacchanalian associations but their disapproval was overridden by its usefulness, for if it grew on the wall of a house the inhabitants were safe from witches. If it withered disaster could be confidently anticipated. In Wales this was said to mean that the house would pass into other hands, either through infertility and lack of heirs or through some financial emergency.

In *Notable Things* Lupton described a procedure in which the enquirer must put an ivy leaf into a dish of water on

Michael J. Barrett

12. Harry Secombe and the 'Four Musketeers' company cutting the Baddeley cake at the Theatre Royal, Drury Lane, on Twelfth Night, 1968 (see page 54).

Little Jack Horner ... *in a corner*
eating a Christmas Pie.

13. This early Christmas card (1872) shows the Christmas nursery
rhyme character Little Jack Horner (see page 25).

Brian Shuel

14. Tolling the Devil's Knell at Dewsbury, West Yorkshire, on Christmas Eve (see page 11).

15. 'Hoisting the Union Jack', by Alfred Hunt, from 'Illustrated London News', December 1876.

Published at Summerly's Home Treasury Office, 12 Old Bond Street, London. From _____

16. (Above)
The first
Christmas card,
designed by
J. C. Horsley,
R.A., for Sir
Henry Cole,
1843 (see page
43).

ALL YEARS LOOK NEW TO HOPE'S UNCLOUDED EYE

17. A Victorian
New Year card.

18. *The dance of Bessy and the Clown was a traditional event on Plough Sunday.*

Hylton Edgar

19. *Tar-barrel burning at Allendale, Northumberland, just before midnight on New Year's Eve (see page 54).*

20. Stories of St Nicholas, the forerunner of Father Christmas, are portrayed in fifteenth-century stained glass at Hillesden church in Buckinghamshire (see page 43).

21. *Mummers at Marshfield, Avon (formerly in Gloucestershire) (see page 46).*

22. *'Twelfth Night', a painting by Jan Steen (1626-79).*

New Year's Eve and leave it untouched till Twelfth Night. If it were green and fresh the coming year would be happy. Black spots foretold illness, in the feet and legs if the spots were near the pointed end, in the stomach or head if they were near the middle, or in the head and neck if near the stalk. General decay could only mean the enquirer's early death. In Oxfordshire a girl would put an ivy leaf into her pocket and go for a walk. The first man she met (even if he were married already at the time) would be her eventual mate. A Scottish variant was for the girl to put an ivy leaf against her heart, reciting:

> Ivy, Ivy, I love you
> In my bosom I put you,
> The first young man who speaks to me,
> My future husband he shall be.

The ivy (*Hedera helix*) was medicinally stimulating, diaphoretic and cathartic, and the leaves were useful for ulcers and abscesses. Corns can be cured by binding ivy leaves in vinegar over them, a vinegar of ivy berries was a popular remedy in the Great Plague of London of 1665 and an ivy wreath worn constantly will prevent falling hair.

Of the minor decorative shrubs and trees, rosemary was holy and magical. It is said to grow upwards for thirty-three years until it is as tall as Christ at the time of the crucifixion and then to grow outwards only. In some districts it, like the Glastonbury Thorn, is said to bloom at midnight on Old Christmas Eve.

The Romans used bay, sacred to Apollo and Aesculapius, god of medicine, and a generally fortunate plant, in their decorations to symbolise fame and fortune. Stow's *Survey of London* mentions its general popularity as a decorative plant. Cypress was associated with funerals and was not liked, yew was used at Easter but rarely at Christmas and was an unlucky plant in the house, but laurel was a favourite church decoration.

The Christmas tree (plate 4), whose introduction is so often attributed to Prince Albert, was in fact known in this country before he arrived. This German custom dates back to the eighth and ninth centuries and the words of a Strasbourg merchant of 1605 are often quoted to demonstrate its early use. 'At Christmas they set up fir trees in the parlour at Strasbourg and hang on them roses cut out of many-coloured paper, apples, wafers, gold-foil, and sweets', and it is linked traditionally with Martin Luther who is supposed to have compared its twinkling candles with the starry heavens on the night of Christ's birth. A member of Queen Caroline's court gave a children's party with a Christmas tree in 1821, but Albert, if not the introducer, was certainly the populariser, and there is no doubt that it rose to its present pre-eminence after Victoria and Albert (a great enthusiast for the customs of his country) included a tree, decorated with candles, tinsel and ornaments in the German manner, amongst their Christmas celebrations in 1841. By 1864 Chamber's *Book of Days* was able to comment, 'Within the last twenty years and apparently since the marriage of Queen Victoria with Prince Albert, previous to which time it was almost unknown in this country, the custom has been introduced into England with the greatest success . . .' In 1854 a huge tree was set up on the site of the 1851 Great Exhibition (Albert's creation) and nowadays part of a London Christmas is to visit the great tree in Trafalgar Square, which since 1946 has been given annually in a very Norse gesture by the people of Oslo (plate 9). The Queen gives two trees to St. Paul's Cathedral each year, one of which stands lighted outside while the other inside is a focal point where the public can leave presents for children and old people. These are representatives of the thousands of trees which decorate churches and market-places all over Great Britain, round which carols are sung. The idea of a communal tree is quite recent and came from the United States where the town of Pasadena, California, set up an illuminated tree on Mount Wilson in 1909. The custom quickly spread across America and then to England.

An older traditional English custom was the Kissing Bough, a double-hooped greenery-covered hoop, with candles, apples, small gifts and ornaments hanging from it, which hung from the ceiling and occupied the pride of place now given to the Christmas tree. Paper decorations seem to have developed only during the nineteenth century when the mechanical cutting of paper became common.

CHRISTMAS CARDS AND GIFTS

Rather refreshingly, for few things about Christmas are so clearly documented, the history of Christmas cards is both short and easily traced. They are very little over 125 years old in the sense in which they are known today.

During the eighteenth century schoolchildren produced 'Christmas pieces' lettered on coloured paper in fine copperplate script to show their parents how they were progressing and to wish them the compliments of the season. The

British Museum has a famous example of a later card, with some claim to be regarded as the first Christmas card, which was produced by William Egley, then about twelve years old, in about 1842, although the precise date is indistinct.

The real instigator seems to have been Sir Henry Cole (1808–82), a Civil Servant and later an organiser of the Great Exhibition of 1851, who suggested the idea of a Christmas card to the artist John Callcott Horsley (1817–1903) in 1843 (plate 16). Whether one should regard patron or artist as the inventor is a moot point. Only about a thousand copies to be sold at a shilling each were printed on this occasion but the pattern was established and the idea swept the world in the next fifty years (plate 13) helped by the introduction in 1840 of Sir Rowland Hill's penny post which at last gave ordinary people the means of mailing greetings to their friends cheaply and easily, and by 1870, when the halfpenny post was introduced for cards and unsealed envelopes, the custom was firmly established with the familiar, sentimentalised scenes of robins, waits, skating scenes and snowed-up mail coaches (perhaps a folk-memory of the great snowstorm of 1836, which brought the mail services of England to a standstill) expressing perfectly that Dickensian good cheer and bonhomie craved by all and actually experienced by so few. These traditional designs spread even to Australia and New Zealand though nothing could be less suitable for countries where the robin is never seen and snow only rarely. In the United States and Canada the poinsettia, discovered in Mexico about 1834, has become an effective substitute.

To the modern mind the giving of Christmas gifts seems to be an off-shoot of the gifts offered by the Magi but it is more probably a survival of the Roman gift-giving (*strenae*) at the *Saturnalia* and *Kalends* celebrations.

Father Christmas, the bringer of gifts, *alias* Santa Claus is derived from St. Nicholas of Patara, Bishop of Myra during the fourth century, whose feast day is 6th December. He is one of Christendom's most popular saints (plate 20), the patron saint of Russia, Aberdeen, parish clerks, scholars, pawnbrokers (because he saved the three daughters of a poor man from prostitution by the present of three gold balls) and of small boys (since he restored three boys who had been cut up and pickled in a salting tub as bacon). From this generally benevolent character was developed Santa Claus and the anglicised Father Christmas, the bringer of gifts by sleigh drawn by reindeer (an American notion, for until the nineteenth century the horse was the accepted animal in England.) He perhaps owes something, too, to his far more adult northern counterpart, Odin, the Old Gift-Bringer, who rode the sky at midnight in winter with his eight-footed horse Sleipnir, distributing punishments to the wicked and rewards to the worthy. By the nineteenth century all these characters had been crystallised into the modern Father Christmas, visitor by night, frequenter of chimneys, resident of Selfridges, joined to his remote ancestor Odin by their common use of a sleigh by night.

It was the custom of the Romans to give gifts to poorer neighbours at *Saturnalia* for which they received garlands in return. At *Kalends* even more gifts were given, many of which had symbolic value, honeyed sweets to ensure a pleasant spirit in the New Year, money or precious metals to ensure prosperity. This custom spread through the Roman Empire although its pagan flavour was frowned on by the early church which cleverly transferred its significance to a ritual commemoration of the gifts of the Magi and shepherds. Perhaps an echo of its true origins can be found in the symbolic offering of bread, money and coal often brought by the First Footers of Scotland and the North of England.

CHRISTMAS GAMES AND AMUSEMENTS

At earlier, less sophisticated Christmases many simple, ingenuous games were played. While the Yule log burned the company dived for apples in a tub of water, jumped for cakes dipped in treacle hung from the ceiling, or jumped in sacks. In the early eighteenth century the author of *Round Our Coal-Fire, or Christmas Entertainments,* wrote, 'Dancing is one of the chief exercises, or else there is a match of Blindman's Buff or Puss in the Corner. The next game is Questions and Commands, when the commander may oblige his subjects to answer any lawful question, and then make the same obey him instantly, under the penalty of being smutted [having the face blacked] or applying such forfeits as may be laid on the aggressor. Most of the other diversions are cards and dice'. Which shows that things have changed very little in two hundred and fifty years.

Snapdragon, with its associations with Scandinavian fire-rites and initiation rituals, was played on Christmas Eve. A quantity of raisins was placed in a large shallow bowl and brandy poured over and lighted. The players tried to grab a raisin by plunging their fingers into the flames and as an accompaniment the Song of Snapdragon was sung:

Here he comes with flaming bowl,
Don't he mean to take his toll
    Snip! Snap! Dragon.
Take care you don't take too much
Be not greedy in your clutch
    Snip! Snap! Dragon.

With his blue and lapping tongue
Many of you will be stung,
    Snip! Snap! Dragon.
For he snaps at all that comes
Snatching at his feast of plums
    Snip! Snap! Dragon.

But Old Christmas makes him come
Though he looks so fee! fa! fum!
    Snip! Snap! Dragon.
Don't 'ee fear him, but be bold—
Out he goes his flames are cold
    Snip! Snap! Dragon.

The lights in the room were put out during the game which was played in the lurid glare from the burning brandy. In the West of England a more economical version of snap-dragon was played, called Flap-Dragon when a lighted candle was placed in a can of cider and the contents drunk by the players, without, if possible, burning themselves, a considerable feat in the days of Victorian whiskers.

Another custom with a clear association with the anarchy of *Saturnalia* was the election of a Lord of Misrule (in Scotland the Abbot of Unreason) to superintend the revels from All Hallows' Eve until Twelfth Night. He was the master of ceremonies who arranged the games and forfeits, the performance of plays and buffoonery of all kinds, drawing everyone into the fun. Sometimes his election was made by the company eating a cake; the person finding a ring in his slice became Lord of Misrule. Stow wrote: 'In the King's house, wheresoever he lodges, a Lord of Misrule, or Master of Merry Disports and the like had ye in the house of every nobleman of honour or good worship were he spiritual or temporal . . .'

At Cambridge University his duties were more serious. In the medieval period and later undergraduates seldom went to their homes during vacations (except in the long summer holiday to help with the harvest) and colleges made arrangements for their entertainment at other times. At Cambridge the Lord (a Master of Arts) superintended the performance of a Latin play (hardly a jolly occasion, one would think)

45

and at the Inns of Court in London the post was particularly splendid for in 1635 this mock ruler spent over £2,000 from his own pocket on the entertainments and was rewarded with a knighthood by Charles I. As a badge of office the Lord had a fool's bauble and was attended by a page in fancy dress who assisted him with his duties. Needless to say this custom was a great butt for Puritan criticism (they were so opposed to Christmas that they even expected Parliament to meet on Christmas Day during the Commonwealth) and the office never recovered from their suppression. Nowadays the paper hats, balloons, forfeits and simple games of the average children's party recapture in some measure the artless spirit of the Lord of Misrule's reign.

Mumming was, and to a small extent still is, an inseparable part of an old English Christmas. The ritual is well over one thousand years old and seems directly linked with pagan rites of the triumph of life over death and with the worship and sacrifices to the Corn Spirit. The players, with blackened faces covered by paper streamers, wore distinctive costumes of strips of paper. The chief characters vary from group to group but a pattern can be detected and the stock characters were often St. George, the Turkish Knight and the Doctor. St. George and the Knight fight and the one killed is revived by the Doctor, dressed in Harley Street manner in top hat and striped trousers (plate 3). At Marshfield, Gloucestershire, it is performed on Boxing Day (plate 21). In Lincolnshire there are characters called Wild Work, Pickle Herring, Ginger Breeches and Allspice and in other plays Little Devil Doubt, Happy Jack, Beelzebub, Oliver Cromwell and even Nelson and Napoleon have made their appearance. As a natural result of a long line of kings, St. George becomes King George in some places. Father Christmas also appears (plate 2), often with the words:

In comes I, Old Father Christmas,
Welcome or welcome not
I hope Old Father Christmas
Will never be forgot.

At Andover, Hampshire, the play was performed until 1963 and was over 800 years old, and other Hampshire plays were given at Longparish and Overton. At Llangynwyd, Glamorgan, the chief mummer wore a horse's skull decorated with ribbons in a rite similar to Mari Lwyd. Revivals of mumming have taken place at Chailey, Sussex, South Cerney, Gloucestershire, and Crookham, Hampshire, amongst other

A party of mummers, from 'The Book of Days' 1864.

places. At Tenby, South Wales, the play ended on a practical note:

> Ladies and gentlemen,
> Our story is ended,
> Our money box is recommended:
> Five or six shillings will not do us harm,
> Silver or copper or gold if you can.

Of this ritual *Round Our Coal-Fire, or Christmas Entertainments* had to say:

> To shorten winter's sadness,
> See where the folks with gladness,
> Disguised are all a-coming,
> Right wantonly a-mumming.

Another traditional entertainment which has only lost its appeal during the twentieth century is pantomime. Its origins are hazy but the Romans had a form of pantomime with the actors performing in mime only and, as they were masked, dependent on bodily movements alone for their effect. Their dress was revealing and when, during the second century, the women began to act naked, the early Christian writers roundly denounced the whole performance.

Nowadays the pantomime is a very British affair but still seems to have some connection with its continental beginnings when a group of French actors, 'Scaramouch, Harlequin, a Country Farmer, his wife and others' complete with performing dogs, first came to England in 1717. By 1758 the famous family of clowns, the Grimaldis, had appeared and at that time the scenic effects took second place to the clowns. Gradually the emphasis changed, the pantomime became a burlesque and extravaganza and finally a sophisticated revue, with a fairy story as a slim thread on which to hang a long performance. *Cinderella* uses part of Perrault's fairy tale with additions from Rossini's opera *La Cenerentola* (with its character of Dandini) and this pantomime is regarded by actors as a lucky one, likely to bring luck to the cast. On the other hand both *Robin Hood* and the *Babes in the Wood* are thought to be unlucky and something unfortunate may occur either during rehearsals or during the run. *Aladdin* is based on a burlesque by H. J. Byron in the 1860s in which the hero's mother was given the name Widow Twankey, derived from the *twankay* which the tea-clippers were rushing home from the Far East for English tea-drinkers. *Mother Goose* is a modern pantomime written for Dan Leno at Drury Lane by J. Hickory Wood in 1902. All these performances, with the other traditional favourites, *Goody Two-Shoes, Bluebeard* and *Robinson Crusoe,* are perfect vehicles for gorgeous dresses, extravagant effects and everything which the stage-manager can devise.

For London children *Peter Pan* is another essential part of Christmas. By Sir James Matthew Barrie (1860–1937), the Scottish novelist and dramatist, it was first produced at the Duke of York's Theatre on 27th December 1904, with the now world-famous characters of Nana, the dog-nurse, Peter Pan, Wendy, Tinkerbell, the flying fairies, Captain Hook, the pirates Smee and Starkey, and the crocodile with the eight-day clock inside him. Authorities such as Sir Henry Beerbohm Tree thought Barrie was mad to hope for success but the author's confidence was fully justified and the play has been produced steadily each year since then with each succeeding generation as an audience. The line spoken by Peter, 'To die will be an awfully big adventure', was quoted by Barrie's friend, Charles Frohman (the theatrical manager who was responsible for first producing *Peter Pan* in 1904), as he plunged to his death in the wreck of the *Lusitania,* 1915.

CHRISTMAS CAROLS

The word carol comes from the Old French *carole,* a dance with a song, and has only been associated with religious celebrations since the fourteenth century, before which carols were sung on any jolly occasion of feasting, dancing or celebration. The great age for English carol composition was from 1400 till 1650 when the Puritans characteristically suppressed them. After the Restoration of 1660 they recovered some, but never all, of their old popularity.

For two hundred years carols were the songs of the very simple and unsophisticated and in 1826 William Hone in his *Everyday Book* condescendingly wrote 'they are ditties which now exclusively enliven the industrious servant and the humble labourer'. Later in the nineteenth century the Victorians, in their eager search for the traditional Christmas of an older England, took them up and a revival followed. Some new carols, in the most regrettable Victorian idiom, were added to earlier collections. Cecil Sharp, the great collector of English folk-song, was responsible for rescuing a number known only through an oral tradition.

In their earliest years carols seem to have been ring-dances and Stonehenge, once called the Giants' Dance, was also known as the Giants' Carol. This pagan entertainment was handed on to the Christian church. The earliest printed collection of carols appeared in 1521 by Wynkyn de Worde and included the famous Boar's Head Carol, still sung at Queen's College, Oxford, and elsewhere. A number of popular carols certainly contain pagan symbolism: *The Holly and the Ivy,* for example, expresses the male/female association of the plants and preserves the pre-Christian fertility significance when both men and women sang and danced together in a mating ritual.

Most well-known carols sung today are of recent origin. The words of *While Shepherds Watched Their Flocks by Night* are by Nahum Tate (1632–1715) and were printed in 1700 although the tune is older and comes from Este's *Whole Book of Psalms* of 1592. The earliest traceable date for both the words and music of *O Come All Ye Faithful* is 1743.

Charles Wesley (1707–88) wrote the words of *Hark the Herald Angels Sing* in the form of *Hark, How all the Welkin Rings, Glory to the King of Kings,* which appeared in its modern form when George Whitefield published his collection of hymns in 1753. The tune, by Mendelssohn, was adapted from his *Festgesang* written in 1840.

Waits, or carol singers, in Yorkshire during the nineteenth century.

The words of *Christians Awake! Salute the Happy Morn* are by John Byrom (1691–1763) and in his diary he wrote, 'Xmas. 1750. The singing boys and Mr. Wainwright came here and sang *Christians Awake*', so the carol, of which Mr. Wainwright was the composer, seems to be firmly datable.

O, Little Town of Bethlehem, by Bishop Phillips Brooks (1835–93) was written for his Sunday School in 1868. The words of *In the Bleak Midwinter* are by Christina Rossetti (1830–94) and the tune by Gustav Holst, written in 1906.

J. M. Neale's carol *Good King Wenceslas* has made this saint's name a household word in England and probably the most familiar to those who have had to endure the persecution of children's carol-singing in the weeks before Christmas. The story told in the carol is purely imaginary although Wenceslas was famous as a Bohemian prince and martyr (c. 907–29). John Mason Neal (1818–66) was an author with High Church ideas and writer of hymns of which this is by far the best known.

Improbably, *It Came Upon the Midnight Clear* owes its

tune to Sir Arthur Sullivan, who took the first four lines of a traditional melody, added four lines and printed it in *Church Hymns,* 1874, of which he was the editor. The words, by E. H. Sears (1810–76) were printed in the *Christian Register* for December 1850 and had been written in the previous year.

The visit of the Waits was once an inseparable part of Christmas. No one now knows if the term originally applied to the musical instruments they carried, the music they played, or the players themselves, but by the mid-nineteenth century it had come to mean the group of musicians who toured the town in the night during the weeks before Christmas. Usually they played wind instruments and any popular music of the day, not necessarily carols, and after a performance money or drinks were expected from the householders. In London the post of Wait was open to purchase and in Westminster the appointment was under the control of the High Constable and Court of Burgesses, which suggests its profitable character.

In Pickering, Yorkshire, two groups of Waits tour the town visiting different parts on the same night, during the week before Christmas, led by a 'shouter'. In the early hours of the morning they approach each house calling 'Good morning, Mr. Brown. Good morning, Mrs. Brown. Happy Christmas to your household! Past two o'clock and a fine morning'. The householder then comes to his door or window and carols are sung; sometimes the Waits receive a hospitable drink before moving on to the next house. This clearly shows the derivation of the Waits from the eighteenth-century watchmen, who developed this sideline over the Christmas season. Once they carried a variety of instruments, serpents, clarinets, fiddles and sometimes handbells as well. A similar custom was common in Devon when the choristers of the parish church, armed with lanterns, went round singing and collecting funds to be used for a feast on Twelfth Night.

Some carol services are world famous. The best known is the Festival of the Nine Lessons and Carols held at King's College, Cambridge, on Christmas Eve, familiar to millions of radio listeners since it was first broadcast in 1930. The chapel, perhaps the greatest ornament of Cambridge architecture, was built by order of Henry VI, founder of King's College and Eton, and the music is of the highest standard. Nine lessons are read, each by a different reader, and nine carols are sung by candlelight including the famous solo performance of *Once in Royal David's City* which opens the service. The choirboy who is to sing this solo is never told until shortly before the service starts. The service was first held in 1918 and is now so popular that one must arrive early in the day to secure a seat.

Almost as famous is the Carol Service, again of Nine Lessons and Carols, held in York Minster at 4 p.m. on Christmas Eve, for which, again, an early arrival is essential.

BOXING DAY

By Boxing Day some of the excesses of the modern Christmas have passed and the many meets of hounds, racing events and sporting fixtures seem to be a direct link with the old feast of St. Stephen. For some reason not fully explained St. Stephen (who died c. A.D. 33), whose feast is 26th December, was connected with horses and his grave at Norrtalje was a place of pilgrimage to which sick horses were brought. John Aubrey in the latter half of the seventeenth century wrote, 'On St. Stephen's Day, the farrier came constantly and blouded all our carthorses'. This was a common and widespread custom; the horses were first galloped, then ceremonially fed and decorated and bled to give them good health for the coming year. This may be a shadowy recollection of earlier horse sacrifices. Many packs of foxhounds meet on Boxing Day, with the accent on the meet rather than the hunt. Typical is the traditional meet of the Whaddon Chase Foxhounds in the market square at Winslow, Buckinghamshire, when the church bells are rung.

The name Boxing Day is said to be derived either from the alms-boxes in churches which were opened on the day after Christmas or by the pottery boxes carried round by apprentices which were filled by philanthropic householders and later broken open to pay for a feast. This form of present-giving has no association with the presents exchanged by relatives and friends and is merely a form of recognition of employees and those who have rendered services in the past year, tradesmen, dustmen or newspaper boys. In the nineteenth century, in an age of less general social equality, these gifts had more significance and postmen, policemen, lamplighters and crossing-sweepers were included as well. Country estates sent gifts of game to those who had rendered even the smallest service and today firms present their employees with the Christmas bonus.

At Drayton Beauchamp, Buckinghamshire, an old custom took place regularly until the nineteenth century. The villagers would visit the rectory and demand as much bread, cheese and ale as they could eat, at the rector's expense. One rector,

52

an economical old bachelor, decided to stop this extravagance and ignored the knocking, hiding with his housekeeper inside the house. One of the unwelcome guests glimpsed him through a window and within a few minutes ladders were raised, the tiles stripped from the roof and nearly one hundred people were ransacking the rectory for every crumb of food and drink they could find. The custom then continued again until 1808 when rioting and drunkenness reached such proportions that it was discontinued and a money payment made in lieu. It finally lapsed about 1827. At Cumnor, Oxfordshire, the tithe-payers expected to receive their bread, cheese and ale at the vicarage on Christmas Day.

NEW YEAR

New Year's Day is full of promise of fresh beginnings and preserves, too, the Saturnalian wish for an alteration in the accepted pattern of life. Bells are rung, sirens sounded and whistles blown to celebrate its arrival and resolutions, sadly soon to be broken, are made.

In Scotland the New Year celebrations outstrip Christmas and the big ritual of New Year's Day is First Footing. The first person, the First Footer, to enter the house uninvited on New Year's Day, and often carrying symbolic gifts of bread, salt, coal and money and perhaps a piece of evergreen, brings good luck in the New Year. Requirements are strict: it must be a man, dark-haired, not flat-footed or cross-eyed and preferably a stranger. In Lancashire for a female to be the first to enter the house was to let in bad luck for the coming year. It is most important to begin the New Year as you would like it to go on: have plenty of money in the pocket, dine well, rise early, pay your debts and lend nothing.

In Scotland it was the pleasant custom to include the animals and give extra feeds on New Year's morning. Burns' farmer in the *Auld Farmer's Address to His Mare* said:

> A guid New-Year, I wish thee, Maggie!
> Hae, there's a ripp to thy auld baggie.

as he gave her extra corn.

New Year celebrations included the ubiquitous wassail-bowl (plate 11)—again filled with lambswool. The word is derived from the Saxon phrase 'Wass Hael'—good health! The Gloucestershire wassail singers after toasting the master and mistress of each house sang:

Here's to Fillpail* and her long tail,
God send our master us never may fail,
Of a cup of good beer: I pray you draw near,
And then you shall hear our jolly wassail.
Be here any maid, I suppose here be some:
Sure they will not let young men stand on the cold stone,
Sing hey, O Maids, come troll back the pin,
And the fairest maid in the house, let us all in.

At Drury Lane Theatre, London, an especially interesting little ceremony takes place on Twelfth Night when the theatre attendants in their eighteenth century uniforms carry a large iced cake in the Green Room. This is provided from the interest on £100 in three per cent funds which was left by the actor-chef, Robert Baddeley, in 1749. Baddeley was the original Moses in *School for Scandal* and it was while dressing for this character on 19th November 1794, that he fell dead. The cake is eaten in his memory every Twelfth Night (plate 12) by the company playing at the theatre, which itself is of historical interest and has a royal box in which every monarch since Charles II has sat. The provision of this cake may recall the once-popular Twelfth Night cake, as well known as Christmas cake is today.

At Wick in the north of Scotland the Old Year is ceremonially burned out with great bonfires round which the people dance and lighted torches are carried in procession. At Stonehaven the custom of Swinging the Fireballs continues, in which flaming balls of paraffin-soaked rope within wire-netting are swung round at the end of cords. Lavish hospitality of all kinds and the giving of special cakes takes place and in some areas the farmers fire their guns to shoot the Old Year.

Another of the most interesting surviving customs is Burning the Clavie at Burghead, Morayshire, at about 6.30 p.m. on Old New Year's Eve, 11th January. The Clavie is half a tar-barrel fixed on a pole called the Spoke. The tar filling is lighted with a brand (matches are never used) and the burning Clavie is carried round the town in a procession led by the Clavie King. House-doors are left open along the route and on the top of nearby Doorie Hill the Clavie is fixed to an old Roman altar. It is then hacked to pieces by the Clavie King and his men and the burning fragments are scrambled for by the crowd as good luck charms to be put up the chimney to bar witches and evil spirits.

At Allendale, Northumberland, the New Year is welcomed with tar-barrel burning (plate 19). The young men of the

* (the cow)

54

town, called 'carriers', balance lighted tar barrels on their heads and proceed to the unlit bonfire just before midnight. The burning tubs are tossed on to it, the bonfire blazes and then with dancing and singing the men become First Footers and the fun goes on till daybreak.

In South Wales on New Year's Day the young men of the villages drew fresh spring water and went from house to house sprinkling all they met (for a few pennies) and would, if required, sprinkle those still in bed.

At St. Ives in Cornwall the Guise Dancers with blackened faces still dance in the street in the first fortnight of the New Year, rather in the manner of the Helston Furry Dancers. At one time they entered the houses too, and for a house to be overlooked was regarded as very unlucky.

At Queen's College, Oxford (which seems to have been lucky enough to preserve a number of its old customs), the Bursar distributes needles threaded with coloured silk to the Fellows after dinner on New Year's Day, with the words 'Take this and be thrifty'. This is based on the English translation of the French pun, *aiguille et fil* on the name of Robert de Englesfield who founded the college in 1341.

Farmers' thoughts turn to their spring ploughing and ploughs are still brought into some churches to be blessed and prayers are offered for the farming community on 'Plough Sunday', the Sunday nearest to 5th January. This ceremony is held at 6.30 p.m. in Exeter Cathedral and at 2.45 p.m. in Chichester Cathedral (plate 5).

On 6th January, the Feast of Epiphany, a service is held in the Chapel Royal, St. James's Palace (which the public may attend), to commemorate the gifts of the Three Kings at Bethlehem. The Queen is represented by two Gentlemen Ushers who make offerings of frankincense, myrrh and gold on her behalf. The gift of twenty-five gold sovereigns is converted into notes and distributed to the aged poor, the frankincense goes for church use and the myrrh to a hospital.

This is the end of Christmas, decorations are taken down, the lights are put out and the *sod. bicarb.* replaced in the medicine chest. Life returns to normal for eleven months until it all begins again and perhaps Charles Lamb may be allowed to have the last word: 'Every first of January that we arrive at, is an imaginary milestone on the turnpike track of human life: at once a resting-place for thought and meditation, and a starting point for fresh exertion in the performance of our journey. The man who does not at least *propose to himself* to be better *this* year than he was last, must be either very good or very bad indeed.'

INDEX